Prisms of War

By Joe Labriola

Published by Schulman Press

Prisms of War / Joe Labriola

ISBN 0-9740728-0-X

FIRST EDITION

Prisms of War

Lynnette Kathleen

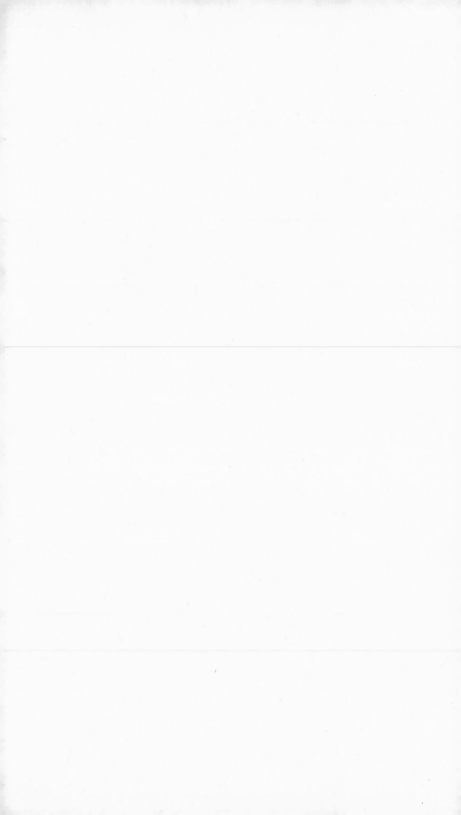

This Book Is Dedicated to
Major Lynnkat
Who Gave Me Reason
for My Next Breath
with the
Courage of Her
Convictions

Acknowledgements

I want to thank the following people and entities for having the effect on my life in the creation of this book:

The United States Marine Corps; my mother Elsie, funniest woman who ever lived; Major Lynnkat; Ruth who badgered, cajoled and steered me toward living my *cursillo* for which I will be eternally grateful. Thanks to Kathleen, the general who always rated a salute; Jim LaPierre who never failed me, above and beyond the call of a friend. To the prison library where I read every book while doing over 18 years in The Hole; prisoners I met along the way — some scholars — and most who demonstrated qualities I am happy not to have. To guards who made my life miserable on a daily basis but never made me lose faith in myself, and guards who proved their humanity despite the depravity we were all subjected to. To Karen who believed and made this book a reality. To Misha, the alpha female who howls at the moon and tells the world to "kiss my hass." To Maurice, "James Bond" slated for canonization for being married to Misha for more than 33 years. To deprivation, segregation, and precious rare silence. To time itself for allowing me the privilege of introspection and meditation. To those heroic Marines and other servicemen and women who gave the last full measure of devotion. To the ability to forgive myself and others. For the absence of hatred and the light of hope instilled by so many I met along the pathways of this life. To Melanie for so eloquently allowing me to see the world through her eyes. For Elizabeth and Chris for giving me a grandson named Taylor and a title I will always be too young for. To Mary who married me and got a raw deal for her love. Back then I still had one foot in the jungle and the other cemented in the mire of self-loathing brought on by survivor's guilt. For the gift my mother passed on by enabling me to laugh — especially at myself — and to believe that the past shapes the future and that maybe — just maybe — we can leave a piece of wisdom in the form of a poem that will instruct others on the horror of war. To myself for eviscerating my soul and allowing it to bleed on these pages. For Big Mike LaCivita, the toughest father-in-law and a fellow poet. To Peter for being there. For Barbara Haggerty for allowing me to walk in her shoes even though they're too big for my feet. For love I felt unworthy to be the recipient of. For God, whatever his or her name may be. And finally to my old pal Bugs Bunny who once counselled: "Don't take life too seriously, because you'll never get out of it alive."

— Joe Labriola
November, 2002

Introduction

I first met Joe Labriola in 2001. At that time Joe was a prisoner in the State Prison at Walpole, Massachusetts. He was introduced to me by my dear friend Misha Defonseca-Levy. She had been visiting Joe for some time and asked me to accompany her on one of her routine weekly visits. I had no idea what to expect nor do I believe that I entertained any sort of preconceived notions. All I knew was that Joe had been in prison for almost 30 years and that he was serving life without parole for murder.

Of the 30 years in prison, Joe has spent over 18 of them in segregation. He rebelled against the system from the very day he entered prison in 1973 and continued to assert his individuality despite the severe consequences that was the "hole." Joe continually made attempts to escape every time he was let out of the hole.

While he was in Norfolk Prison, Joe got elected to Chairman of The Norfolk Lifers Group and also Commander of The Veterans in Prison group. He combined the efforts of both to initiate a voters drive because Massachusetts was one of only five states where prisoners were allowed to vote. He felt he could demonstrate to the younger prisoners that they would be able to accomplish more with ballots than with bullets. He also was part of a small group of men who formed the first Political Action Committee behind bars. The story of this appeared on the front page of The Boston Globe. Then governor Argeo Paul Cellucci ordered the guards to lock those men up and confiscate all their "political materials." This triggered a ballot referendum, and within two years the vote was taken away from prisoners by an act of legislation.

Joe organized the other prisoners into collecting soda cans in all the different areas where they would get a 5-cent deposit on return. With over 1200 prisoners they were able to raise hundreds of dollars which all went to various charities. The Lifers Group also had the ice cream shack when prisoners were still allowed to buy ice cream. With the profits from that shack and a captive bunch of consumers, the Lifers Group raised thousands of dollars that also went to charities. When these worthy charities began writing letters about the decency of these lifers, the ice cream shack was taken away. Once again Joe was put in the "hole." Joe is now in the Super Maximum prison at Souza/Baranowski Correctional Center in Shirley, Massachusetts, where he is working on a book based on his prison experiences.

Prior to prison, Joe was a disabled veteran who attended Glassboro State College in Glassboro, New Jersey, where he was on the Dean's List. He was going to college under the G.I. Bill of Rights. Joe served with distinction with the 1st Marines in Vietnam and was awarded the Bronze Star Medal with Combat "V" and Purple Heart for saving the lives of his men while under fire and seriously wounded himself. However, if you ask Joe, he will tell you right away that there is no such thing as heroes in war.

Joe was Honorably Discharged from the Marines with a small pension. He has written extensively about his "misadventures of youth" in combat and has written a series of poems on the subject, some of which appear in this book.

Recently I read Joe's trial transcripts and was struck by something the judge in his case said to the jury (and this is a direct quote) "Now, in this particular case, the case of Commonwealth *vs.* Labriola, if this case is to be proved at all, it is to be proved by circumstantial evidence because it is not suggested that any direct evidence can be given or any witness can be called to give testimony...." During the trial in 1973, two full years before the war in Vietnam ended, and when almost everyone in America had an opinion about Vietnam — mostly all negative — Joe was grilled by the Assistant District Attorney while on the stand: "Is it true, Mr. Labriola that you served in Vietnam?" "Isn't it also true that you killed lots of people?" "Isn't it true that to someone like you, killing is no big deal?" "That's what you were trained for, right?" The Assistant District Attorney did not so much ask these questions as he literally screamed them at Joe. The judge halted the trial, made the Assistant District Attorney apologize to Joe, and then asked the jury to strike the entire exchange from their minds. That was sort of like throwing a skunk into the jury box and asking them to disregard the odor.

With not a single eyewitness, without anyone coming forward to say they heard Joe admit to the crime, without a single shred of forensic evidence whatsoever, the jury came back with a verdict of guilty. How could they possibly have reached this conclusion? The victim in this case was a career criminal who was killed with his own gun, which was found lying next to his body and the only fingerprints on the gun belonged to the victim himself. In reading these transcripts, one can only surmise that Joe became a victim of a tumultuous period of time in American history and had his excellent military record turned around to be used against him instead of showing what a brave and honorable Marine he was. To say here that I am shocked and angry would be a gross understatement.

At this writing Joe continues to appeal his case. He is on the last leg of the appeal right now and has no faith in the system. He told me once that all he wanted was to make sure that someone knew what happened to him in case he should die in his cell. Now I know. Now you know. Yet, I choose to believe in hope — that somehow the truth will prevail and Joe will be a free man, able to return from the horror that was war and three decades of prison.

— August, 2002

Anyone wanting to know more information about Joe can contact me at:

Karen Schulman
PO Box 84
Hopedale, MA 01747

Foreword

I first met Joe Labriola six years ago while giving a speech in Norfolk prison where Joe was incarcerated at that time. I immediately recognized in him his leadership qualities. I further learned that Joe received the Bronze Star Medal with Combat "V" for heroism along with a Purple Heart Medal and several other commendations.

I was in WWII and we both saw in each other not only the physical wounds, but also more importantly, the invisible and terrible wounds that were much later termed to be Post Traumatic Stress Disorder (PTSD).

We exchanged hundreds of letters and I better came to know this man who sacrificed his youth in the jungles and rice paddies of Vietnam. A war fought primarily by teenagers.

I have since visited Joe once a week and found a man with a rare heart and a generosity of spirit with a marvelous gift for writing. I saw him suffering from the loss of his young wife and I saw him still suffering the loss of his comrades in war. But I saw him laugh as he made me laugh, and where there is that kind of laughter at life's ironies, there is hope.

Joe is incarcerated for a crime he has consistently denied committing. He writes stories and he writes poetry — some of which you will read in this book — that so vividly describes love, war, and life's sufferings.

Joe is one of the rare people to whom I would trust my very life.

He is a man of honor.

He is my friend.

I salute this Marine.

— Misha
Author

Contents

THE WAR POEMS

THE BUSH

We awoke to the sound
of helicopter blades swooshing
and parting the grass in circles.
Dawn came up fast, too fast.
The light burned tired eyes
as we locked and loaded
wondering what hell awaited today.
The praying lamp was lit
for those who still had Gods
while the Sargeant checked quietly
making sure each man had ammo.
Nothing more needed to be said.
Nothing more could be said.
It was a day for killing.

19 YEARS OLD

It was two days I figure
before I knew for sure
those were your bone fragments
stuck in my matted hair
mixed with sweat and blood.
Streaks cleaned my cheeks of mud
straight lines off my stubbled chin
as salt burned in my eyes
I still believed in God
and said a silent prayer
mixed in with a lot of why's
Your destiny was to die in Vietnam
while mine was to never come home

RUNNING WITH THE SUN

I ran with the sun
alone, blood on my chest
with last night's flashes
still stinging tired eyes.
I left you in the rice paddie
after dragging you for miles
cause I loved you — and mom
would want your body home
clean of all dried sweat
and wearing your high school face
lying beneath the glass top
with that sleeping look
painted on by mortician magic.
Why only yesterday
after so many years
of swallowing too many pills
and passing out in beer mugs
or crying alone at odd times
when strangers and friends alike
would walk away or around me
that I wish it was never
a memory more painful
than any hell I've ever known . . .

SOLDIERS IN THE MUD

I cried somewhere
between arms and legs
hearts and souls
of boys my age
and men even younger
not looking at all proud
in death.
I cried somewhere
from a shadow world
of ancient warriors
that understood my water.
I cried somewhere
because men like us
had to lead the world
by the example
of our tears . . .

WAR BABY

You never blinked
as the raindrops
beat into your wide open eyes.
Sitting in the cover
of a sugarcane field
I watched and became
a wartime philosopher.
I made confirmations
about life and death,
war and peace.
In the distance
I heard a mother screaming
for her baby.
Is it you she calls?
Is your spirit aware?
Does it know
that by me killing you
I also killed a part of myself?
I sat there in the monsoon rain
with the rifle between my legs
and my chin resting on my knees
staring at the rain in your eyes
thinking about how
the rice paddy mud of war
is a lonely place to die.

HEROES

There are no heroes in war.
Just frightened little boys
teasing the neighbor's dog
with branches of trees
much too big
to be handled effectively.
Just men who think they are right
and will murder your entire family
to prove just how right they are.
There are no winners in war.
The award for first or second place
are scars mounted on bloody walls
hanging in the dens of minds 'til death
and all too sadly, beyond.
There are no heroes in war.
It was just that acting brave
was a hell of a lot easier
than being scared.

TIME DOES NOT HEAL

Augie was killed by a sniper
bullet in the ass — exit the gut.
Francis J. August, warrior brother,
foxhole comrade who shared dreams
and hopes of life back in the world.
My life saver, my courage, my friend.
I have seen you since breathing your last . . .

I have seen you in Malcolm
I have seen you in Martin
I have seen you in Medgar
I have seen you beaten in Selma
I have seen you bitten in Birmingham
I have seen you hanged in Mississippi
I have seen you bleed on foreign soil . . .

I have seen that look in my eyes
a thousand yard stare in a five foot room.
Shaving an older face I have seen your sadness.
I have seen you in me — as me — your image
like crystals in my tears
I have seen you . . .

MEMORIAL

They're there every year
multi-clad and beribboned
beneath faded bush hats
carrying long distance scars so proudly
in weathered Asiatic eyes
staring ahead at some personal sound
like thunder from the inner ear
and little children tugging grenade pockets
wanting to know,
"What did you do in the war, Daddy?"

The parades were too late
and the angry streets too silent
in mock reverie to wasted youth
who climbed on and were carried off
too many planes head and feet first
while the whole world watched
Walter Cronkite at six o'clock
over Cheerios and Big Macs
seeing reality as another sick sitcom
in blood color
up close and impersonal . . .

WAKE NIGHT

They've all gone home, Kenny . . .
There were a lot of people
from your high school . . . .
Mothers, fathers, sisters, brothers,
and some veterans groups
class of '45 wearing
campaign hats of varying colors
with emblems of patriotic servitude,
and every one of them saluted
as they passed by in respect
to the full measure you gave.
I stood at Parade Rest,
full dress blues with medals,
NCO sword all polished,
cover pulled low to my eyes,
my guts on fire, and my head
jammed with grief.
They've all gone home, Kenny
but I'm still here with candles
burning their perfume smells
knowing for us both,
there will never be a night like this . . .

KENNY'S FLAG

Mrs. Miller I remember
the look that passed between us.
There were leaves on the ground,
tears in our eyes.
Your son, my brother, is dead.
The flag folded properly
showing only the blue field.
My job was to stand tall
and present it to you.
I was a hard sargeant then
I mean —
presenting the flags should be routine
except —
I'm allergic to Taps.
My speech was;
"Mom, this flag
is what Kenny lived by,
believed in, and died for."
The look we shared
said something else.
Had a boy Marine died
for a liar's victory?
We called on God.
Even He was silent that day.
Mrs. Miller, wasn't it quiet that day?

ANOTHER BROTHER FALLS

Another brother falls
in a different war
far from home
on a battlefield
in his own mind
where demons
danced
behind eyes
in midnight slumber
of tortured dreams
of a haunted soul
in a sweat soaked bed
heart pounding
silently praying
for dawn's first light
as fear
made his skin crawl
oozing from every pore
overpowering
his mortal soul
no longer able to pretend
that life was good
as he took his own
permanently healing
his heart
while wounding
all loved ones
left behind.
Another brother
called by death
alone and proud
to the end
to say good-bye
Semper Fi
as grown men wept
and wondered
why . . .

RIO's PTSD

The wind whistling
shaking the window
over the drumming sound
of rain on an aluminum sill
like the roof of a quonset hut
near the airstrip in DaNang.
He clings to the bedpost
sliding in sudden sweat
dragged like a runaway slave
back to the jungle
he was once lucky enough to escape
with minor and major wounds
from other teenagers' weapons
many years — only yesterday ago.
Squeezing his eyes tightly shut
or trying to remember songs
sung in a crackling voice
never stopped the flight
into the combat/twilight zone
of I Corps vines and canopy,
great leeches, water Boos,
trip wires, circular grave mounds,
clearing by fire, cold C rats
of ham and motherfuckers, fields of bodies,
shouts of "INCOMING" followed
by panic screams of "CORPSMAN UP,"
and of all those smells,
burnt gunpowder and blood
from bitten lips
to stifle the screams
long distance from his youth.

THE PRISON POEMS

PEOPLE LIKE ME

Got some Double Bubble to chew
so I won't break more teeth gritting
at the images assaulting my sensibilities.
the smell of rotting meat,
mine, theirs, and the shit they feed us.
I wake up nights swinging at shadows
and roaches who want to eat my lips.
Cigarettes taste better in the dark
and the salt from my tears sweeter
than the ones I shed in anger
at the chains I cannot break.
Sometimes I lay fetal for hours
listening to Clarence building another nest
in the cardboard box beneath my bed.
The little bastard shredded three poems,
one disciplinary report, and a book marker.
The screws shine flashlights hourly in my face
but I don't blink anymore.
I can hear paint drying on the walls,
steam pipes banging, fungus growing
and something larger than a mouse in my trash bag.
Sometimes my old war wounds ache so bad
that I want to cry out for my mother
except she died long distance a few years ago
and besides — us hardened convicts
laugh at people like me . . . .

BENJO DITCH BLUES

Benjo ditch coffee
starts the morning
getting internal motors
functioning like train wheels
on a vaselined track
and there ain't nothin'
like the final sound
of metal on metal
as unseen doors are slammed
open and closed
to the melodic tune
of onward cell soldiers
beating in the lithium minds
of small thinking men
who own the now,
sustained by the yestedays,
surviving for the tomorrows,
waiting to trade in their number
for the name
they left at the front desk.

INDIGO NIGHTS

The face glowed its light
and in the dark I watched
the crystal showing your eyes
and smiling your O'Joe smile.

There was a pause
after rising to my feet
and padding naked to the window
where softly I spoke your name.

The bars left vertical stripes
on my powerless heart
and the taste of blood
on lips so recently kissed.

I felt your life's breath
softly on my cheek
where evening dust made mud
when mixed with eye water.

There were moon shadows
and star memories
of all that we have been
in penitentiary promises.

This night was made for lovers
to speak their fire
and howl their passions
to a heaven that has not heard it all . . .

SUSTENANCE

I see her drawing closer
with long wind combed hair
head held so high and proud.

I know her so well . . .

In her steps I see her moods
and in her voice when she greets me
I hear the things she doesn't say.

I feel the same pains
through the same pleasures
when finally our eyes meet
and the sparkling beams bore
my soul
like that of a child
as he reaches for his milk.

I will not go hungry this day . . .

EMOTIONAL ENEMY

My companion
loneliness
laughs at me
from every corner
of every room
stalking me in every step
it lurks in silence
like wafts of sinister breaths
trying to break my spirit
in the stillness of the night
my strength comes
in moments remembered
by your side
your love burns within my heart
and I know
at least until tomorrow
I have conquered this emotional enemy
surviving one more night
alone . . .

SACRIFICES

Your eyes could always talk
through the stillness of silence
between us on wishing days
as we sat in plastic chairs
among hostile and lonely strangers
unconcerned with our blood.

Your hand could always touch
places so deeply hidden
from the face of God or man
because you were stronger than both
and had the life-death grip
of a woman in love.

Your mind could always pierce
the armor of my caged and wild heart
or see so deeply into my darkness
even when I pushed you toward the light
of nonexistent tomorrows
without me.

THE VISITING ROOM

Amidst the drab walls
of yellow-brown interior
decorated with steel doors
of gray
lay years of whispered conversations
saddened hours
of hands held too tightly
of smiles
lost to hearts and souls
that long to soar
in freedom
years of struggle
to maintain
a quiet serenity
in a room created
for human tears
screaming outrage
in silent agonies
and in eyes that no longer sparkle
dying slowly from too many good-byes
Heartbreak is written
like graffiti on city streets
as souls, too weary, fall
exhausted
from all the sessions of sadness
and loss
they have been witness to . . .

SURVIVING THE PAIN

Yesterday's pain
got buried
in a hole deep in the earth
after the reasons for it
were uncovered
discovered, categorized
and accepted as another part of life
I turned around
and wondered which pocket
do I place today in
What compartment
does tomorrow get filed under
and where will there be room
for all the infliction to come
when the mind's landfill
can no longer contain it
Amidst the wasteland
of broken dreams
stolen moments
and images lost to years
each one, ever so precious
now gone and buried
within the ruins of our love
I grow afraid of the dark once more
knowing they've found a way
to take you from me again
and the pain of fresh wounds
fester with time
knowing our only defense
is the invisible line
connecting our two hearts
as we survive new atrocities
other men's minds
create for us to endure . . .

BEYOND

Beyond the wall
of stone and wire
Beyond the clouds
and all we can touch
Beyond the trees
and all the world's wrongs
Beyond the horizon
and all we can see
in our eyes
through our dreams
There is a place for us
Beyond the way of life
as we know if for now
There will be love
and we both
will finally understand . . . .

THE BIG C

You are a feather quill poet
living in a ball point time
dreaming all your what if's,
how it should have been's,
licking swollen lips,
puppy eyes, milk moustache
momma cat.

The big C's kicking ass,
making you talk to God,
keeping your head up,
smelling wind-washed air,
seeing colors in the rain.
Ain't it a bitch now momma,
I mean, ain't it a bitch.

THE LOVE POEMS

SUNSET EYES

Rain falls gently
on the window
where I stand
with visions of you
hearing voices of laughter
and your words
pressed softly against my ear
as eternities pass
in waiting for life
in a place
where all days begin
in the sunrise of light
in your eyes
and never have to end
in the sunset of your tears . . .

ONLY UNTIL

I will love you
but only until tomorrow
when the tomorrow never comes.
I will hold your hand
but only behind closed eyes
that sign our separation.
I will speak warm words
but only after I swallow
the lump of my lonely being.
I will lick the air
but only when the moon is full
and yours is the face in it.
I will wait at the river's edge
but only when my chains have shed
and my ribs swing out
showing me the glow of your heart.

CLOSE AS I AM

If I had a tail
it would drum the floor
as I saw you approach
each and every day.
I'd lick your hand
and nuzzle your lap
letting you stroke my head.
I'd cry and whimper
like a frozen animal
saved by your warmth.
I'd sleep on your feet
protecting you from everyone
and everything.
I'd love you
with the fiercest loyalty
and be almost as close
as I am now
to your heart.

GUTLESS BASTARD

My life was spent in hiding
all the tears I now share with you
unafraid to let you run barefoot
in the cellar of my battered soul.

My life was spent in keeping
memories of bloody foreign jungles
buried in top secret graves
that I refused to recognize.

My life was spent in torture
because I never had a reason
to tell you then what I tell you now,
I WANT TO LIVE!

PEACOCKS

Men fell to their knees
in the middle of your song
as come-on beams shone
from the emerald of your eyes.
I know, I was one of them.

Lines were drawn and feathers unfurled
open for your appreciation
of we pretty cocks impressing
the best of our colors.
I know, mine were the rainbow.

We strutted our stuff upon the stage
of youth none of us understood
and pretended to be what we thought we were
imagining only what we might be when we grew up.
I know, I was the most immature.

Men danced across your path
hoping for your recognition and nod
while I captured, sat in a cage
feeling my buckshot soul and dum-dum heart.
I know, for I loved the you in you.

NO TURNING BACK

The heat of your skin
sent shocks through my hands
and filled my lust with thoughts
of things that used to be.

I remember you in youth
and nights of breathless whispers
when getting old did not exist
nor with us could ever be imagined.

The touches of then
made food for separate journeys
and water to wash away the salt
from faces needing to be held.

Bells tolled in our maturity
as we grew from war to peace
and made promises easier to keep
for this our chosen love
there was no turning back.

THE GUIDE

Freedom lingers before me
teasing like a smoke ring
and through the round hazy hole
framed, I see your smiling face.

I close my eyes and hear you
in the distance of light years
where you have been waiting
to taste the promises of my dreams.

In over thirty years of chains
I've stood defiantly tall
and never bowed my head
nor felt man's cement beneath my knees.

I see around the corners of tomorrow
and with an inherent jungle instinct
long before the collision of karma
I am ready for your touch.

How I have worshipped you
and drawn deeply from your strength
waiting for the day to come
and your guiding hand to lead me home.

STEEL HORIZON

The rain on the window
like sand on the sill
was part of happy days
wishing myself to the mountain
to climb a hobbled horse
waiting to be lathered
along old elk trails
over rocky streams
down deep gullies
to the place you live
and to the embers
of your ruby heart
that stood watching
a steel horizon
for the cowboy spirit
closing the distance.

SIX TIMES SEVEN

I despise my humanity
and all its frailties
with errors in judgment
making wrong choices
when feeling disjointed
to the only love
I have ever known.

I hate my jealousies
and conjured suitors
I see hiding everywhere
in jackal packs
waiting for the kill
of the lonely prey
trying desperately to survive.

I pity the people
who point out more
about some magic
that does not exist
when their own lives
are no shining example
held up to scrutiny.

I apologize out loud
for all my maleness
that seems to overshadow
the truer gifts inside
and all the beautiful touches
I am unable by iron bars
to deliver in time.

I pray for that tomorrow
and another chance to show
that love is worth it all
in waiting through the pain
and suffering in silence
that my kiss can heal
more than it can kill.

I fall on bleeding knees
with reverential awe
palms upraised toward the ceiling
and whispering through the food slot
to my wife so far away
in a prison of her own
I love you, Lynnette Kathleen.

GIFT OF THE GODS

I never had anything of my own
except my soul pure on my sleeve —
not even a God in which I could believe.

The Gods I knew seemed angry and determined
as I lived through mines, bullets,
sweat, blood, and too many tears.

They gave you to me my love.

They gave you to me so I would believe
in someone besides myself.

They gave you to me so I would cry
in revelation of my mortal self.

They gave you to me for I was worthy
of love granted to make-believe heroes.

They gave you to me for they knew
I would love and protect you with my life.

They gave you to me because I needed you
when I screamed at heaven that I needed no one.

They gave you to me in a single kiss
that changed my life forever.

TEST TEMPERED

My pugilist arms
grew too heavy to hold
up against the blows of life
and my ring tactics had to change
in order to survive the fight
of the brutal violent arena
that was my razor-wire existence.

I saw you in the crowd
through the blue-brown haze
of the non-smoking section
and your bright green eyes
beseeching me to climb through
to where you white-knuckle waited
for my hard fought victory.

Bloody and scarred
I would come to you alone
on feathered feet
and fire wings forged in war
test tempered by challenge
to break so many chains
secured by people
foolish enough to bet against us.

WHEN YOU NEED ME

When you need me
I will always be there
inside your heart
where I have lived forever.

When you need me
I am the smile in your eyes
and the reflection in your mirror.

When you need me
I am the hero in your novels
and the slayer of hidden dragons.

When you need me
I am your dreams
and the fire of your desires.

When you need me
I am the manna
feeding your hopes.

When you need me
I am there . . .

THE SEA

There was a fire in the sky
posing innocently as the sun
burning my non-blinking eyes
staring across worlds of oceans
made of your laughter and time.

I could not turn away or bend
blistering lips to salty knees
or touch my face to the sand
wet with tears beneath my feet
and slowly pulled away by tide.

There was music in the moment
and voices of morning gulls
that formed in spelling circles above
a life filled with breezes
and whispers of promises made in clay.

I would wait and check my breath
cracking whips to tame the lion heart
roaring thunder at the center of the world
and lapping crashing waves of screams
for its missing mate, my love, the sea.

I KNOW

I know
the heart
that beats
within your own breast
for it beats within mine.
I know
the mind
within your being
as if each thought
and reasons for them
were my own.
I hear
the words you say aloud
and those you whisper softly
when we're together
or when you're alone
in the middle of the night
and cannot sleep
for they are spoken
from my lips too
and I am sleepless with you.
Every tear you've shed
I've shed as well
for I know
and I understand you
and most of all
I love you
and I understand
you love me too.

BELIEF

It was your heart
that gave me life
when mine was frozen
cut off resolutely
from the world of love.
It was your courage
that inspired my muse
when words of beauty
hid themselves so well
from my trembling hand.
It was your eyes
that made me see
when I refused to feel
anything but emptiness,
and gave me strength
for belief in tomorrow.

Lynnette K. Labriola, RN
January 12, 1953 – September 18, 2001

THE LAST VISIT

I failed
because
I could not touch
her face
or kiss her
pale lips
through the security glass
and bad light
seeing
my own reflection
as her tears
were my tears
and together
in our own way
we faced
certain death
for her at home
with Sam the cat
in her fading arms
and mine
alone
in a prison cell.